The Hide and Seek Squirrels

Written by Lari Don

Illustrated by Deborah Partington

Collins

Hazel, Cashew and Conker gathered a large batch of acorns for winter. They hid them in a secret spot.

Hazel whispered, "Let's draw a picture on a leaf to help us find our acorns."

"That's nutty!" shouted Cashew. "Let's put a huge stone on the hole."

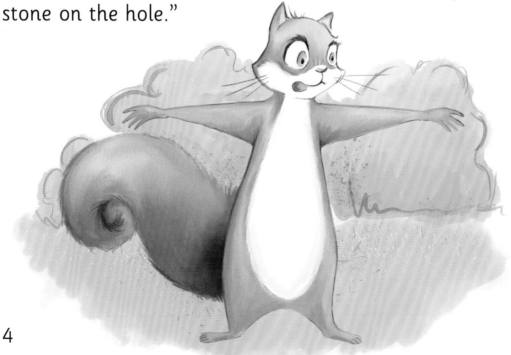

"That's a fluff-tailed idea!" said Conker. "Let's make up a song."

There was a chorus of shouting.

"The leaf would get lost!"

"We couldn't push a giant stone!"

"We'd forget the song!"

The squirrels flicked their fluffy tails in rage.

Hazel scratched a picture on a nearby leaf.

Cashew searched for a large stone.

Conker devised a song.

By the oak tree,
step ahead three.
Lunge to the right ...
for a nutty delight.

9

When it grew chilly, they met to fetch their acorns. But Hazel's picture had blown away.

They only found beetles under Cashew's stone.

Conker's song led to a puddle ...

Hazel's tummy growled.

Conker was hungry and had no energy.

Cashew panicked – how would they survive the winter?

"Your acorns were here," said a little squirrel above them, pointing triumphantly at a hole.

Hazel, Conker and Cashew whirled round and leaned over the edge ...

... but the hole was empty.

"Where are our acorns?" asked Cashew.

"I hid them somewhere else," said the little squirrel.

"That's not fair. Those are our acorns ..." cried Conker.

"You couldn't work together, so you lost the acorns.
I found them by myself," said the little squirrel.

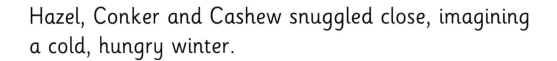

Hazel, Conker and Cashew snuggled close, imagining a cold, hungry winter.

The little squirrel paused, considering a cold, lonely winter. "I have plenty of acorns, but nobody to share them with ..."

So all four squirrels shared the acorns.

They played hide-and-seek. It was simpler finding each other than finding hidden nuts!

21

Finding the acorns

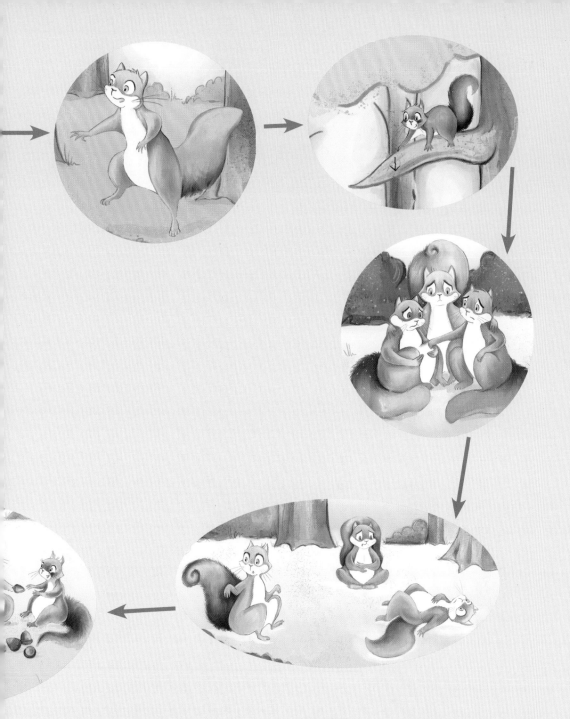

After reading

Letters and Sounds: Phase 5

Word count: 299

Focus phonemes: /ai/ a /j/ ge, g, dge /ch/ tch, t /ee/ e, y /w/ wh /c/ ch /s/ se /igh/ y, ie /l/ le /f/ ph /v/ ve /oo/ u /z/ se

Common exception words: of, to, the, are, said, were, our, their

Curriculum links: Science: Animals, including humans; PSHE

National Curriculum learning objectives: Spoken language: use relevant strategies to build their vocabulary; Reading/word reading: apply phonic knowledge and skills as the route to decode words; Reading/comprehension: understand both the books they can already read accurately and fluently and those they listen to by predicting what might happen on the basis of what has been read so far, making inferences on the basis of what is being said and done

Developing fluency

- Your child may enjoy hearing you read the book.
- You could each read the part of one or two of the squirrels. Talk about how the speech marks tell us that a character is talking.

Phonic practice

- Ask your child what this letter sound is: /c/. Say it together a few times.
- Now read page 6 to your child. Ask them to listen out for the letter sound /c/. When they hear it, ask them to repeat the word to you. (*chorus, couldn't*)
- Look at the word **couldn't** together. Ask your child which letter stands for the letter sound /c/. (*c*)
- Now look at the word **chorus** together. Ask your child which letters stand for the letter sound /c/. (*ch*)
- Talk about how the same letter sound can be written in different ways.

Extending vocabulary

- There are lots of interesting verbs in this book to describe the actions of the squirrels. You may wish to remind your child that a verb is a doing word.
- Look at page 2 together. Point out some of the verbs. (*gathered, hid*)
- Now look at pages 8 to 9. Ask your child to point out the verbs. (*scratched, searched, devised, step, lunge*)
- You could add actions to the verbs.